W9-AYK-838

100 Unforgettable Moments in
Pro Hockey

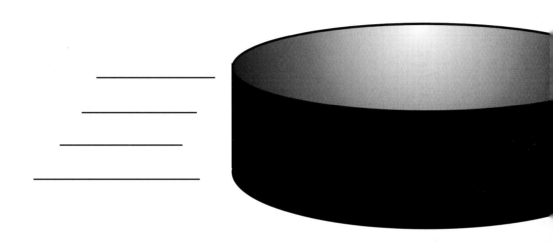

Bob Italia

ABDO & Daughters
Publishing

Published by Abdo & Daughters, 4940 Viking Drive, Suite 622,
Edina, Minnesota 55435.

Copyright © 1996 by Abdo Consulting Group, Inc., Pentagon
Tower, P.O. Box 36036, Minneapolis, Minnesota 55435 USA.
International copyrights reserved in all countries. No part of this
book may be reproduced in any form without written permission
from the publisher.

Printed in the United States.

Cover Photo credits: Allsport
Interior Photo credits: Wide World Photo

Edited by Paul Joseph

Library of Congress Cataloging-in-Publication Data

Italia, Bob, 1955-
100 unforgettable moments in pro hockey / Bob Italia.
    p. cm. — (100 unforgettable moments in sports)
  Includes index.
Summary: Describes notable events in the history of pro hockey
and the National Hockey League.
ISBN 1-56239-691-9
1. Hockey—History—Juvenile literature. [1. Hockey—History.]
I. Title. II. Series: Italia, Bob, 1955- 100 unforgettable moments
in sports.
GV847.25.I83 1996
796.962—dc20   96-33874
                                                    CIP
                                                     AC

Contents

The Most Unforgettable Moment?

The National Hockey League (NHL) has had a long history filled with many unforgettable moments. Just recently, the New York Rangers ended a 54-year Stanley Cup drought with a dramatic, hard-fought win over the Vancouver Canucks. Then there was Brett Hull's frantic—and successful—attempt to score 50 goals in less than 50 games.

Many of the NHL's most unforgettable "moments" weren't moments at all. Some of these great accomplishments took a season—or a career—to achieve, like the Montreal Canadiens record-23 Stanley Cups, or Wayne Gretzky's all-out assault on every NHL scoring record.

There is no one most unforgettable moment. The following events are in chronological order, not ranked according to importance. That judgment remains in the hands of hockey fans who cherish this exciting, fast-paced sport.

Opposite page: Edmonton Oiler Paul Coffey skates toward the puck against the Rangers.

The NHL is Born

In the early 1900s, battles for control of the National Hockey Association (NHA) grew fierce, mostly because of Edward J. Livingstone, who managed to antagonize every one of his fellow owners. By 1917, they decided that they had had enough of Livingstone. But getting rid of him would be a problem. Livingstone had been a franchise-holder in Toronto and was a NHA member. To rid themselves of Livingstone, the owners would have to create a new league.

In November 1917, representatives of the top pro teams—Ottawa Senators, Quebec Bulldogs, Montreal Canadiens, Montreal Wanderers, and Toronto Arenas—met at the Windsor Hotel in Montreal. Livingstone was kept from the meeting.

When the meeting finally ended, a brand new league had been born: the National Hockey League (NHL). The new NHL consisted of Ottawa, Montreal (Wanderers, Canadiens) and Toronto. Frank Calder was named the league president.

The Wanderers never finished the season. Fire destroyed the Montreal Arena on January 2, 1918. Wanderers owner Sam Lichtenhein tried to borrow players from other teams. When they refused, Lichtenhein withdrew from the NHL.

The Quebec Bulldogs won the Stanley Cup in 1912-1913.

With only three teams, the NHL barely made it through its first season. But the Toronto Arenas became the first NHL club to qualify for Stanley Cup play. Toronto defeated Vancouver three games to two. Corbett Denneny emerged as one of the new league's first stars.

Joe Malone

The NHL became a success because of one man: Joe Malone. Malone starred for the Quebec Bulldogs in the National Hockey Association. When Quebec folded, the Montreal Canadiens signed him. In 1917-18, Malone scored 44 goals in 20 games.

Malone would have stayed with the Canadiens after the 1918-19 season. But Quebec rejoined the NHL in 1919-20 and reclaimed him.

Quebec did not do well in 1919-20. They finished with a 4-20-0 record and gave up twice as many goals as they scored. Malone was one of the team's few bright spots. In a game against the Toronto St. Patricks, Malone scored seven goals—an NHL record that has never been equaled. Malone's scoring ability made headlines across Canada, which helped the three-year-old NHL gain in popularity.

Opposite page: Joe Malone of the Quebec Bulldogs, early 1900s.

The NHL Comes to America

By its seventh season, the NHL caught the attention of several American promoters, who arranged games to be played in U.S. cities. In the early 1920s, the NHL had become a hit in Boston. It was only a matter of time before an NHL franchise came to Beantown.

New England grocery magnate Charles F. Adams was convinced that the NHL couldn't miss in the United States. After gaining a new NHL franchise for Boston, Adams hired Arthur

Ross to manage the team. Ross signed players for the new club. On December 1, 1924, the Boston Bruins became the first U.S. team in the NHL.

Boston opened with a win over the Montreal Maroons—the year's other expansion team. Then they lost 11 consecutive games. The Bruins finished the season with a 6-24 record, eight points behind the Maroons. Boston scored just 49 goals and gave up 119. Lionel Hitchman and Alf Skinner were the top players.

Despite their difficulties, the Bruins won the hearts of Boston. The NHL's expansion into America became a big success. Franchise applications poured in from other American cities.

When New York's Madison Square Garden was completed, a bid came from a group of businessmen in Manhattan. At the same time, another application came from Pittsburgh. Hockey had made it in America. The NHL's first great expansion boom was about to begin.

Opposite page:
The Boston Bruins
of the 1920s.

The Rangers Win the Cup

There have been many instances where starting goaltenders have been hurt during a game and replacements performed brilliantly in their place. But one of the most famous episodes involved New York Rangers coach/manager Lester Patrick in the 1928 Stanley Cup Finals.

Entering Game 2, the Montreal Maroons led the series 1-0. After a scoreless first period, Montreal center Nels Stewart blasted a shot that struck Rangers goalie Lorne Chabot above the eye, knocking him from the game. Without another goalie on the bench, Patrick was forced to play goal—a position he had never played in his life.

When the 44-year-old Patrick took his position, laughter erupted from the Forum crowd. But they were soon silenced as the Rangers built a human wall in front of their goalie, who stopped 15 of the Maroons' 16 shots. At the end of regulation, the game was tied 1-1.

With seven minutes to go in the overtime, the puck slid behind the Maroons' goal. Rangers defenseman Ching Johnson intercepted it. Frank Boucher was stationed in front of the net and yelled for the pass. Ching pushed the puck to Boucher who knocked it into the net. The Rangers had scored one of the most amazing victories in NHL history.

For Game 3, Patrick started goalie Joe Miller, whom he borrowed from the New York Americans. Montreal won the third game 2-1. But Miller came back in Game 4 to post a 1-0 shutout. New York took a 2-1 victory in Game 5, clinching the series. Had it not been for Patrick, Montreal would have taken the second game—and probably the series. Even more, it was the first time a U.S. team had won the Stanley Cup.

Lester Patrick, 1928.

Heroic Charlie Gardiner

Although the Chicago Black Hawks had been in the NHL since 1926, they had very little success. But in 1933-34, goaltender Charlie Gardiner changed their fortunes as the Hawks gave up the fewest goals in the league (83). Gardiner posted an amazing 1.73 goals-against average—including 10 shutouts.

Unknown to everyone, Gardiner was suffering from a tonsil infection that was slowly killing him. It didn't matter to Gardiner. All he wanted to do was win the Stanley Cup.

The Hawks made it to the Stanley Cup Finals where they played the favored Detroit Red Wings. The best-of-five series opened in Detroit. The Black Hawks stunned the Red Wings by taking the first two games.

As the series returned to Chicago for Game 3, experts conceded the Stanley Cup to the Black Hawks. But Gardiner was playing with pain, and Detroit won 5-2.

As Gardiner took his place in the goal crease for Game 4, his body was still in pain. But for two periods, he did not give up a goal. In the third, Detroit captured the momentum and seemed ready to break the 0-0 deadlock. But Gardiner held them scoreless. The game remained tied at the end of regulation. Now Gardiner would have to play into overtime.

Charlie Gardiner.

Gardiner weakened as the game went through the first overtime and into the second. Despite his pain, Gardiner held Detroit scoreless halfway through the second overtime.

At the 10-minute mark, Chicago's Mush March skated into Detroit territory and fired a shot at Redwing goaltender Wilf Cude. The puck whistled past Cude and into the net before he could make a move. The Black Hawks had won their first Stanley Cup. Two months later, Gardiner died in a Winnipeg hospital.

The Greatest Overtime Game

Overtime hockey is one of the most exciting events in sports. Every shot can bring sudden death to one team, sudden victory to the other.

The greatest overtime game in NHL history took place on March 24, 1936, at the Montreal Forum. It was the first game of the semifinal series between the Maroons and the Detroit Red Wings.

Despite the scoring talent on both teams, neither club scored a goal in regulation, sending the game into sudden-death overtime. Goaltenders Norm Smith of Detroit and Lorne Chabot of the Maroons turned back all shots through five sudden death periods. Four minutes and 46 seconds after the ninth overall period began, the teams broke the NHL record for the longest game.

The veterans of both teams were exhausted. Younger skaters had to take their place on the ice. One of them was 21-year-old Modere "Mud" Bruneteau. During the 1935-36 regular season, he had scored only two points. But Red Wings coach Jack Adams knew that Bruneteau had the most energy.

After the 16th minute of the sixth overtime, Bruneteau took the puck into the Detroit zone and passed it to a teammate who shot it across the blueline. Bruneteau skated behind the Detroit defense, retrieved the puck, and shot it past Chabot.

Referee Nels Stewart put up his hand to signal the goal. After a complete game and 116 minutes and 30 seconds of overtime, the Detroit Red Wings had defeated the Montreal Maroons 1-0.

Modere "Mud" Bruneteau.

"Sudden Death" Hill

The first NHL player to score three overtime playoff goals in a career was Mel Hill—and he scored them all in one series. The 25-year-old Boston Bruins forward performed his sudden-death magic in the 1939 playoffs.

The best-of-seven series opened at Madison Square Garden in New York. After regulation, the teams skated to a 1-1 tie. No goals were scored in the first or second overtime periods.

By this time, Boston coach Art Ross had noticed how New York was shadowing high-scoring left wing Roy Conacher, allowing him few shots. Before the third overtime, Ross decided to build a play around Hill. At 19:20 of the third overtime, Hill got his shot. The Bruins won the game.

In Game 2, the teams were tied 2-2 at the end of regulation. Eight minutes into the first overtime, Hill took a pass—and scored another game-winning goal. The series moved to Boston, where the Bruins scored an easy 4-1 victory in Game 3.

The Rangers refused to give up, surprising the Bruins with three straight victories. Game 7 turned into another sudden-death affair as the teams went into a third overtime tied at 1-1.

Eight minutes later, Hill took a pass and fired a shot past Rangers goalie Bert Gardiner. The puck found the net—and the Bruins won the series, four games to three.

Boston breezed past Toronto four games to one in the Stanley Cup Finals. But the performance of "Sudden Death" Hill was the talk of Beantown.

Forward Mel Hill (left) after scoring three "sudden death" goals to win the series.

The Greatest Comeback

In the history of professional sports, only once has a team overcome a three-games-to-none deficit in the final series to win the championship. It happened in the 1942 Stanley Cup Finals between the Toronto Maple Leafs and the Detroit Red Wings.

The faster Red Wings squad surprised Toronto with two victories at Maple Leaf Gardens. Then they won 5-2 at Olympia Stadium in Detroit for a seemingly insurmountable three-games-to-none lead.

Toronto had to make dramatic changes if they wanted to compete for the Cup. They benched their best scorer, Gordie Drillon, and replaced him with forward Don Metz. Defenseman Bucko McDonald was pulled in favor of rookie defenseman Ernie Dickens.

The changes worked wonders in Game 4. After falling behind 2-0, the Leafs rallied for a 4-3 win as Metz set up the winning goal.

Game 5 was played in Toronto. Metz was the star as he scored a hat-trick and added two assists during a 9-3 Maple Leaf rout. The series returned to Detroit for Game 6, but Turk Broda blanked the Red Wings 3-0. Now the series was tied 3-3. Game 7 would be played in Maple Leaf Gardens.

Detroit opened the scoring with a goal by Syd Howe. But the Maple Leafs answered with a Sweeney Schriner power play goal. Toronto then scored two minutes later on a goal by Pete Langelle.

The Wings began to panic. They charged the Maple Leafs with little concern for defense. As a result, Schriner knocked in another goal. When the horn sounded, Toronto had a 3-1 victory. It was the greatest comeback in hockey history.

Toronto Maple Leaf Pete Langelle.

The Rocket Scores 50

In 1945, the Montreal Canadiens were the team to beat. The man to stop was Maurice "Rocket" Richard.

"He can shoot from any angle," said Boston goalie Frank Brimsek. "You can play him for a shot to the upper corner and the Rocket wheels and fires a backhander to the near, lower part of the net."

Though Richard had all the offensive tools, his desire to win made him the ultimate scorer.

"When he skated in on the net," said Hall of Fame goalie Glenn Hall, "the Rocket's eyes would shine like a pair of searchlights. It was awesome to see him coming at you."

One of Richard's most impressive accomplishments came in 1945. That's when he scored 50 goals during the 50-game season. The following year, Richard scored 45 goals—establishing the Rocket as the NHL's first offensive superstar.

Opposite page:
Maurice "Rocket" Richard.

The First Hockey Dynasty

When the Toronto Maple Leafs beat the Montreal Canadiens for the 1946-47 Stanley Cup, it was regarded as a fluke victory. Leafs owner Conn Smythe was determined to build a better team and silence his critics once and for all.

Toronto had two great centers, Syl Apps and Ted Kennedy. If the Leafs could get one more, their strength down the middle would make them the best.

To reach their goal, Toronto traded the youthful and talented line of Bud Poile, Gaye Stewart, and Gus Bodnar—as well as highly regarded defenseman Bob Goldham and 1942 Cup hero Ernie Dickens—to Chicago. In return, they received 1946-47 scoring champion Max Bentley.

The trade was the biggest in hockey history. It transformed the Maple Leafs from a good team into a hockey machine.

"It was the best Toronto team I ever had," said Smythe, who had operated the Leafs since 1927. "Bentley gave us strength down the center and was the final piece of the puzzle."

Bentley played some of his greatest hockey for the Maple Leafs as Toronto finished the 1947-48 season with a 32-15-13—good for first place. In the semifinal playoff series, the Leafs defeated Boston four games to one—then rolled over the Detroit Red Wings in the Finals.

Detroit was no match for hockey's greatest team. Toronto swept Detroit in four straight—including a 7-2 thrashing in the finale. With two straight Cups, the Maple Leafs were on their way to building a dynasty.

Toronto Maple Leafs (white uniforms) fire a shot on goal.

Five Overtime Games

As the 1951 playoffs began, NHL fans anticipated a Stanley Cup Finals meeting between Detroit and Toronto. Instead, it was Toronto and Montreal in a series that would become the most dramatic of all time. Toronto reached the Finals by defeating the Boston Bruins, while Montreal stunned the heavily-favored Detroit Red Wings.

The Finals opened at Maple Leaf Gardens. The game went into overtime tied 2-2 when Toronto's Sid Smith beat goalie Gerry McNeil to give the Leafs a one-game lead.

Game 2 was another overtime affair. This time, Montreal came away with the win. In the third game, Maurice Richard gave Montreal the lead. But Smith tied the score 1-1. For the third straight game, the teams entered overtime.

Within the first four minutes, the Canadiens penetrated the Toronto defense three times. But each time, they were turned back. Finally, Toronto's Ted Kennedy scored the game-winner for a 2-1 series lead.

The series switched to the Montreal Forum. Fans wondered if the overtime trend would continue. Never in Stanley Cup history had there been four consecutive overtime games. But a goal by the Canadiens tied the game at 2-2, setting up the record-breaking extra session. Toronto's Harry Watson knocked one in to give the Leafs their third sudden-death victory.

It seemed impossible that five straight Finals games would reach overtime. With Montreal nursing a 2-1 lead late in Game 5, it appeared the streak was over. But Toronto scored with 32 seconds remaining, setting up a fifth straight overtime game.

Like all the overtimes, this one ended quickly as the Leafs' Bill Barilko scored at 2:53 to win the Cup for Toronto. Never had the NHL experienced such a dramatic—and sudden death—Finals series.

Bill Barilko (falling) scoring for the Maple Leafs in the Stanley Cup.

Jacques Plante Arrives

Never in hockey history has a goalie revolutionized his position like Jacques Plante. Plante aided his defensemen by skating from his goal crease to retrieve pucks that skidded behind his net—which in his day was never done.

Plante introduced his style as a rookie in 1953 when the Montreal Canadiens battled Chicago in the playoffs. Montreal coach Dick Irvin used veteran goaltender Gerry McNeil. But when the Canadiens fell behind in the series 3-2, he decided to try his inexperienced rookie.

In his first playoff game, Plante shut out the Black Hawks 3-0. With Plante in goal, Montreal then won the series-clinching seventh game, and cruised past Boston to win the Stanley Cup. In four playoff games, Plante had a 1.75 goals-against-average.

Plante remained a backup in 1953-54. But when he played, he was brilliant. By the 1955-56 season, Plante had become the NHL's best goaltender. The Canadiens strolled to the regular-season title with a 45-15-10 record—24 points ahead of second-place Detroit. Four of the top seven scorers came from Montreal. Jean Beliveau, Maurice Richard, Doug Harvey, and Plante were named to the First All-Star Team. Plante's 1.86 goals-against-average earned him the Vezina Trophy as the NHL's top goalie—his first of five straight and sixth overall.

In the playoffs, the Canadiens cruised past the New York Rangers and the Detroit Red Wings to win the Cup. Montreal beat each team in five games as Plante earned a 1.80 goals-against-average.

Plante's success with his unique style inspired other goaltenders. In November 1959, he became the first NHL goalie to wear a mask. Soon, other goaltenders began wearing face protectors of their own. By the late 1960s, goalie masks became standard equipment—all because of Jacques Plante.

Jacques Plante, Montreal Canadiens' goalie.

Toronto's Late-Season Run

In 1958-59, the unheralded Toronto Maple Leafs came out of nowhere to earn a playoff berth and reach the Stanley Cup Finals. This was a season in which the Canadiens were shooting for their fourth straight Stanley Cup and would easily finish first. The Canadiens were so strong that fans only wondered who would finish second.

To make the playoffs, Toronto had to hope that another team would collapse. No one expected that team to be the New York Rangers. They had finished in second place a year earlier. New York started to falter early in March. But they were still nine points ahead of Toronto on March 11 and seven points up on March 14.

New York had its chance to knock Toronto back in the standings. A Ranger victory would give New York a nine-point lead over Toronto. With four games remaining on their schedule, the Leafs could never make up the difference. But the unexpected happened. Toronto won back-to-back games against the Rangers.

On the final night of the season, the Leafs needed a win in Detroit and a Rangers loss at Montreal to take the playoffs. In their game, the Rangers blew a lead and lost to the Canadiens 4-2. Toronto rallied from a two-goal deficit to defeat the Red Wings 6-4.

Toronto's amazing surge continued against Boston in the playoffs. The Leafs won two overtime games. Then, in the decisive seventh game in Boston, they surprised the Bruins 3-2. The streak ended quickly in the Stanley Cup Finals, as the Canadiens whipped the Leafs in five games. Despite the loss, Toronto's late-season run remains one of the most amazing in NHL history.

The Toronto Maple Leafs against the Boston Bruins in the 1958-59 playoffs.

The Greatest Team Ever?

The Montreal Canadiens had won a fourth straight Stanley Cup in 1959. During the off-season, Manager Frank Selke made some minor changes. But the championship team remained together.

The following season, Montreal had its challengers. The Chicago Black Hawks were rebuilding their team around emerging superstar Bobby Hull, who scored 81 points in 1959-60 to end Dickie Moore's two-year reign as scoring champion. Chicago also had Glenn "Mr. Goalie" Hall, and a top-notch defense, anchored by Pierre Pilote and Elmer Vasko.

But the Hawks lacked Montreal's depth. Eight future Hall of Famers played for Montreal, including Maurice and Henri Richard, Boom Boom Geoffrion, Jean Beliveau, Dickie Moore, Doug Harvey, Tom Johnson, and Jacques Plante. With all their superstar talent, the Canadiens finished the 1959-60 season with a 40-18-12 record.

The Maple Leafs also threatened Montreal after Toronto obtained Red Kelly from Detroit. Toronto finished in second place, then defeated Detroit in a six-game semifinal series. The Canadiens, meanwhile, swept Chicago in four semifinal games.

Toronto used a heavy-checking game in the Finals, but could not knock Montreal from their game. The Canadiens engineered another four-game sweep and skated off with the Stanley Cup. The victory confirmed what everyone had already known: Montreal was the greatest team the world had ever seen.

The Montreal Canadiens win another Stanley Cup.

A Hart for Howe

In the 1962-63 season, 34-year-old Gordie Howe was outplaying opponents a dozen years younger. Howe scored his 500th career goal in March 1962, then took aim at Maurice Richard's record of 544. No one in the league could skate, stick-handle, and shoot better than Howe. For his efforts, Howe won the scoring title—and his record-sixth Hart Memorial Trophy as the league's Most Valuable Player.

Despite Howe's great season, Detroit finished fourth. But Howe led the Wings to a semifinal playoff upset over the Chicago Black Hawks. In the Finals against the Maple Leafs, the Red Wings lost in five games.

Howe continued to outplay his younger opponents. In 1964 and 1965, he made the All-Star Team. Howe would make six more All-Star trips by 1970, giving him 22 career appearances. Howe didn't retire until 1980 when he was 52 years old—34 years after he first joined the NHL.

Opposite page:
Gordie Howe (#9) battles
for the puck against the
Toronto Maple Leafs.

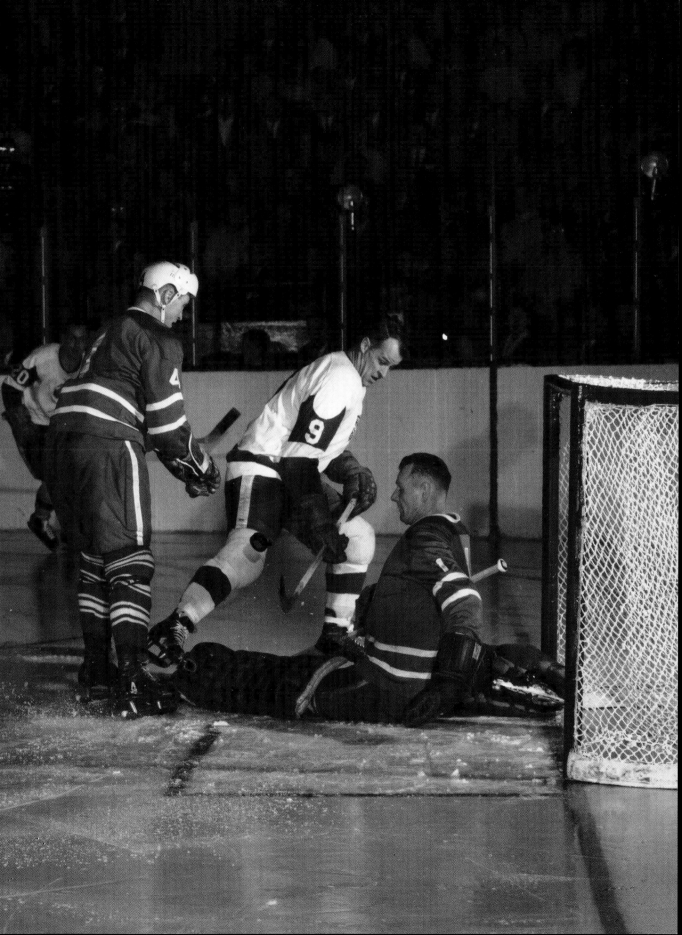

Shining New Stars

In 1963-64, two of the most talented men ever to play in the NHL—Frank Mahovlich and Bobby Hull—began to dominate the league.

Hull skated for the Chicago Black Hawks. He was called the Golden Jet because of his blond hair. But Hull also had blazing speed—and a cannon-like slapshot that was feared around the league. The mere sight of Hull winding up to shoot intimidated even the most experienced goalies. As if his slap shot weren't enough, Hull's mighty legs and powerful arms enabled him to withstand body-checks that would have crumbled lesser players.

Toronto's Mahovlich was not as flashy. But once on the ice, the "Big M's" smooth strides gave him great skating power. And his shot was just as thunderous as Hull's. Mahovlich was the star of a Toronto team that had won Stanley Cups in 1962 and 1963.

The Chicago Black Hawks posed the biggest challenge to Toronto in the 1963-64 season. Besides Hull, Chicago had a creative stick-handler from Czechoslovakia who quickly became one of the NHL's best centers. His name was Stan Mikita. In 1963-64, Mikita fought his way to the top of the scoring list.

The anticipated Stanley Cup showdown between the new stars never materialized as Chicago was upset in the playoffs. Instead, Mahovlich's Leafs and Gordie Howe's Red Wings battled for the Cup. The series went to seven games before Toronto captured the title.

The presence of these new superstars sparked more interest in hockey. Other major cities bid for teams of their own. Bowing to the pressure, the NHL began laying plans for expansion. The NHL would never be the same.

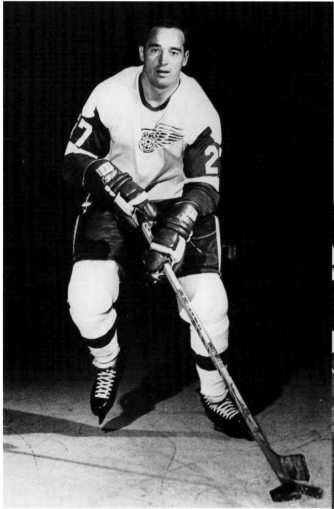

**Frank Mahovlich,
Detroit Red Wings.**

The Golden Jet, Bobby Hull.

Bobby Orr Transforms Hockey

Bobby Orr had the kind of talent that only a few NHL players could ever claim. Scouts noticed Orr before he reached his teens. After watching the 12-year-old Orr play, the Boston Bruins put his name on their protected list.

Orr became a hockey star faster than anyone imagined. By the time he was 16, everyone in Canada new his name. Orr's impact on the NHL would be immediate, as he would help transform Boston into a hockey dynasty. By 1970, Orr would become the biggest star in the game. Even more, he changed the way the game of hockey was played.

Orr's idea of defense was to steal the puck from an opponent, then skate the length of the ice for a shot on goal or a pass to a teammate. Soon, every kid in Canada wanted to be Bobby Orr.

In his rookie season of 1966-67, Orr didn't lead Boston to the playoffs. Still, he won the Calder Trophy as Rookie of the Year. New York's Harry Howell took the Norris Trophy as best defenseman.

At the awards luncheon, Howell accepted his trophy and said, "I am glad I won the Norris Trophy this year, because in 10 years it will be the Bobby Orr Trophy."

Bobby Orr of the Boston Bruins.

David vs. Goliath

Never in NHL history has a team been as terrifying as the 1970-71 Boston Bruins. The big, bad Bruins scored 399 goals for the season—108 more than any other team. Center Phil Esposito lit the lamp 76 times, breaking the NHL record by 18. His 152 points also smashed his own NHL record by 26.

But it was Bobby Orr who stole the show—and the Hart Memorial Trophy as the league's Most Valuable Player. Orr's 37 goals set an NHL record for a defenseman—while his 102 assists were the most ever.

Boston met Montreal in the first round of the playoffs. Nobody gave the Canadiens a chance.

After beating the Montreal Canadiens in Game 1 at the Boston Garden, the Bruins thought they were on their way to another Stanley Cup. When they piled up a 5-1 lead in Game 2, it looked as though the series would be a laugher. But then something unexpected happened: the Canadiens staged a furious rally for a shocking 7-5 win.

Even more surprising, the Canadiens forced the Bruins into a seventh game at the Boston Garden. By now, the Bruin scorers were baffled by the Montreal defense. They had little success in Game 7, which the Canadiens captured 4-2. Montreal went on to beat Chicago in seven games for the Cup. But their defeat of Boston remains one of the biggest upsets in sports history.

Phil Esposito scores a goal, breaking an NHL record in 1970.

From Patsy to Champions

In only two years, the Philadelphia Flyers underwent one of the sport world's biggest transformations. Though a patsy in 1971-72, the Flyers emerged the following season as the most hated, the most respected, and the most colorful team since the 1970 Boston Bruins.

The Flyers banged out a 50-16-12 record in 1973-74, then muscled their way through a six-game Finals series against Boston—becoming the first recent expansion club to win the Stanley Cup.

The Flyers were led by superstar center Bobby Clarke. They also had the NHL's best goalie, Bernie Parent, co-winner of the Vezina Trophy and recipient of the Conn Smythe Award as the Most Valuable Player of the Stanley Cup. Center Rick MacLeish also shined. He scored 32 goals during the season—including the game-winner that clinched the championship.

Bobby Clarke skates in on the defense.

A Record-Setting Team

The 1976-77 Montreal Canadiens were a record-breaking team featuring such stars as Guy Lafleur, Steve Shutt, and Ken Dryden.

Lafleur was the biggest attraction, leading the league in scoring for the second straight year while teaming with the high-scoring Shutt and center Jacques Lemaire. He also claimed the first of two straight Hart Memorial Trophies as the league's Most Valuable Player.

Serge Savard, Guy Lapointe, and Larry Robinson formed a rock-solid defense. Bill Nyrop and Brian Engblom also pitched in well on defense. With the nearly impenetrable wall in front of him, goalie Ken Dryden breezed to his second straight Vezina Trophy as top netminder.

With their All-Star talent, the 1976-77 Canadiens dominated opponents, outscoring them 387-171 for the season. The Canadiens had no trouble defending their 1975-76 Stanley Cup. In the playoffs, they swept St. Louis, then knocked off the Islanders in six. In the Finals, Montreal thrashed Boston in four games, outscoring the Bruins 16-6.

The '75-'76 and '76-'77 Canadiens were more than just a hockey team. They were a finely tuned hockey machine—and perhaps the best the NHL has ever seen.

The Canadiens' Guy Lafleur fires the puck over the shoulder of St. Louis goalie Ed Stankowski.

Gretzky's Scoring Tear

Throughout NHL history, the idea of a player scoring 100 goals in one season seemed laughable. Then Wayne Gretzky stepped to the ice for the 1981-82 season.

A year earlier, Gretzky had scored a league-high 164 points on 55 goals and 109 assists. Some experts thought Gretzky might one day score 65 or 70 goals in a season. But in 1981-82, Gretzky surprised everyone with numbers that were out of this world.

Gretzky quickly shot to the top of the scoring list early—then skated far ahead of New York Islanders' Mike Bossy, who would finish the season with 64 goals. Gretzky scored his 50th goal in his 39th game—making a joke of the 50-goals-in-50-games feat Bossy achieved one year earlier.

"In one stretch of four games," Gretzky said, "I got 10 goals. I had 45 goals in 38 games." On December 30, Gretzky faced the Philadelphia Flyers. "That night," Gretzky continued, "turned out to be one of the greatest of my life."

By the six-minute mark of the third period, Gretzky had scored four times and had reached 49 goals. With time running out, the Flyers were down 6-5. So they pulled their goalie for an extra skater. That gave Gretzky another chance. Glenn Anderson fed Gretzky the puck, and he flipped it into the empty net. Gretzky had scored 5 goals in 1 game—and 50 goals in 39 games. "I knew then," said Gretzky, "that I'd beat Phil Esposito's record of 76 goals in a season."

Gretzky broke the record for most goals in one season in his 66th game. He eventually became the first player to break the 200-point barrier (212). His only "disappointment" was his 92 goals—8 goals short of the 100-goal mark he had hoped to achieve.

A young Wayne Gretzky (99) in an Oiler uniform.

The Islanders Create a Dynasty

Having won three consecutive Stanley Cups, the New York Islanders were as talented as they had been when they won their first title. Billy Smith's outstanding goaltending was made even better by a tough defense. Forwards Bob Bourne, Butch Goring, Bryan Trottier, Mike Bossy, Clark Gillies, and Anders Kallur made up a potent offense.

The Islanders were favored to make it back to the Finals for a fourth consecutive time—and they did. But this time, the Edmonton Oilers and superstar Wayne Gretzky stood in their way. Edmonton finished the season with 106 points and in first place in the Smythe Division. They steamrolled into the Finals for the first time. Most experts picked New York to fall against the powerful Oilers.

Despite their powerful offense, Edmonton was totally outplayed by the Islanders. New York swept the Oilers with their overpowering defense. In Game 1, Smith turned back every Edmonton shot as New York won 2-0. In Game 2, the Islanders scored three goals in the first period and cruised to a 6-3 win.

The Isles easily won Game 3 by a 5-1 score. In Game 4, New York scored three goals within 1:37 of the first period. Then Smith held the score to 4-2 with some great saves.

The New York Islanders became the first U.S. team to win four consecutive Stanley Cups (1980-1983)—and only the third team in NHL history to win four in a row. Smith, who held the Oilers to six goals in the Finals, won the Conn Smythe Trophy as the Most Valuable Player.

Dennis Potvin of the Islanders holds the Stanley Cup triumphantly.

Edmonton Takes Control

During the early 1980s, the New York Islanders were the best in the NHL. Their tough defense helped them win four consecutive Stanley Cups. However, their No. 1 challenger, the Edmonton Oilers, had their own theory on the best way to win a hockey championship. Defense was not in the formula.

The Oilers focused on a high-powered offense that would overwhelm opponents—and they had the talent to get away with it. In 1983-84, Wayne Gretzky scored 87 goals and 205 points. Mark Messier, Jari Kurri, Glenn Anderson, and high-scoring defenseman Paul Coffey also lit the lamp often.

The Oilers were winning a lot of hockey games with this system, but they hadn't won a Stanley Cup. The Oilers knew they had to win it in 1983-84 or the club would be dismantled and a new approach would be tried.

The Islanders remained a tough defending champion through the 1983-84 season. But this time, they struggled through the playoffs before making it to their fifth consecutive Stanley Cup Finals. The Oilers, however, breezed through the playoffs and were favored to win it all.

In Game 1, Edmonton goalie Grant Fuhr made the difference. After Edmonton scored the first goal, Fuhr shut down the Islanders the rest of the way for a 1-0 win. New York rallied to win Game 2, but having won 19 consecutive playoff series, they were beginning to show signs of fatigue. When the series switched to Edmonton, the Oilers took charge. They swept the Islanders off the ice with three convincing victories.

For the first time in his career, Wayne Gretzky hoisted the Stanley Cup. The Edmonton Oilers went on to win four Stanley Cup Championships in the next six years.

Edmonton Oilers Wayne Gretzky waves as he and teammates celebrate their Stanley Cup victory.

Super Mario Arrives

Before 1984, few Canadian junior players had ever caused more excitement than Mario Lemieux. Despite his 6-foot 4-inch, 200-pound frame, the 18-year-old Lemieux was a fast, graceful skater who carried a powerful shot.

Lemieux was the greatest scorer in Quebec Major Junior Hockey League history. In three years, he scored 247 goals and 562 points in 200 games. In his final year, 1983-84, Lemieux scored 133 goals and 149 assists for 282 points in 70 games. Then he added 52 points in 14 playoff games.

Lemieux would go to the NHL team that finished last in 1983-84. The Pittsburgh Penguins won that honor with only 38 points for the entire season.

From the moment he stepped onto the ice for the 1984-85 season, NHL rookie Mario Lemieux lived up to all his lofty expectations as he dazzled the Pittsburgh fans with his offensive skills. Lemieux scored his first NHL goal in his first game on his first shift off his first shot. He was named to the All-Star Game and earned the contest's Most Valuable Player with two goals and an assist. When the season had ended, Lemieux had scored 43 goals and 100 points. Lemieux was the runaway winner of the Calder Trophy as the NHL's Rookie of the Year. Lemieux's sudden stardom led to comparisons with superstar Wayne Gretzky.

As the years went by, Lemieux proved that he was Gretzky's equal. In 1987-88, he outscored Gretzky 168 to 149 while ending the Great One's streak of eight consecutive Hart Memorial Trophies as the League's Most Valuable Player. And while Gretzky would win back-to-back Stanley Cup championships in 1987 and 1988, Lemieux would match that feat in 1991 and 1992. He was now the best player in the NHL.

Mario Lemieux holds up the Stanley Cup.

The Rangers End the Jinx

For decades, the New York Rangers proved that spending money on high-priced players couldn't help them win a Stanley Cup. But finally—decades after they won the Stanley Cup in 1940—the best team money could buy ended their championship drought.

To get to the Finals, New York purchased players such as forward center Steve Larmer and goalie Glenn Healy. They also hired coach Mike Keenan, paying him almost $1 million a year. These players were added to a team that included Brian Leetch on defense and three high-scoring Russians—Alexei Kovalev, Sergei Zubov, and Sergei Nemchinov.

By midseason, the Rangers had taken a firm hold of first place. Captain Mark Messier was playing his best hockey ever and Adam Graves—one of many ex-Edmonton Oilers on the team—was on his way to a 52-goal season. To everyone's surprise, Zubov matured into the club's highest-scoring defenseman.

The Rangers finished with a league-best 52-24-8 record, then opened the playoffs with a sweep of the Islanders, then eliminated Washington in five games. Against the tough New

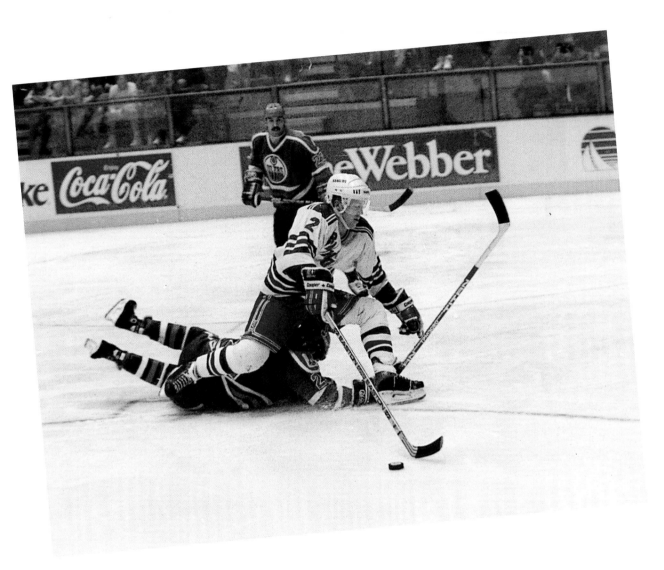

Brian Leetch was the star player on the tough New York Ranger defense.

Jersey Devils, the Rangers won after a hard-fought, seven-game series. That sent New York into the Stanley Cup Finals against Pavel Bure and the Vancouver Canucks.

After losing the opener at home, the Rangers reeled off three straight wins. Fans packed Madison Square Garden for Game 5 in anticipation of a Cup celebration, but the Canucks won 6-3. When Vancouver took the next contest 4-1 to tie the series at 3-3, it looked as though the Finals jinx was about to strike again.

New York fans anxiously watched their Rangers take a hard-fought 3-1 lead into the third period. They gave up one more goal—then hung on for a 3-2 triumph. The players hoisted the Stanley Cup and paraded it around the ice, showing their fans a trophy they hadn't seen in 54 years.

The New York Rangers celebrate after winning the Stanley Cup.

More Unforgettable Moments

1929—George Hainsworth records 22 shutouts.

1937—Davey Kerr records four shutouts in nine playoff games.

1937—The Detroit Red Wings become the first American team to win two consecutive Stanley Cups.

1938—Nels Stewart becomes the first to score 300 career goals.

1939—Roy Conacher becomes the first rookie to lead the league in goals scored.

1941—Bill Cowley racks up a record-45 assists.

1941—The Boston Bruins complete the first-ever four-game sweep in the Finals.

1944—Herb Cain scores an NHL-record 82 points in 1 season.

1944—Clint Smith sets a record with 49 assists.

1944—Syd Howe scores six goals in one game.

1951—Goaltender Terry Sawchuck wins a record-41 games.

1952—Bill Mosienko nets 3 goals in 21 seconds.

Number 21, Stan Mikita.

1953—Gordie Howe scores a record-95 points.

1954—Bert Olmstead scores eight points in one game.

1958—Willie O'Ree becomes the NHL's first black player.

1959—Dickie Moore sets an NHL record with 96 points.

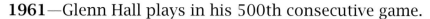

1961—Glenn Hall plays in his 500th consecutive game.

1962—Gordie Howe records his 500th career goal.

1964—Gordie Howe scores his NHL-record 545th career goal.

1966—Bobby Hull becomes the first player to reach the 50-goal plateau twice; also becomes the first player to score more than 50 goals in one season; finishes the season with a record-97 points.

1967—Stan Mikita scores 97 points in 1 season.

1967—Bobby Hull becomes the first player to score 50 goals in 3 different seasons.

1969—Phil Esposito smashes the scoring mark with 126 points.

1969—Bobby Hull scores 58 goals in 1 season.

1970—Bobby Orr sets a scoring record for defensemen with 120 points and 87 assists; also becomes the first defenseman to win the scoring title.

1970—Tony Esposito wins the Calder Trophy and the Vezina Trophy.

Bobby Orr.

1970—Bobby Hull scores his 500th career goal.

1971—Phil Esposito scores a record-76 goals.

1971—Bobby Orr sets an NHL record with 102 assists.

1971—The Boston Bruins score a record-399 goals in 1 season.

1973—Henry Boucha scores a goal six seconds into a game, setting the record for quickest goal in league history.

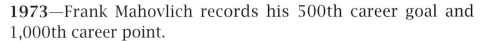

1973—Frank Mahovlich records his 500th career goal and 1,000th career point.

1973—Bernie Parent wins a record-47 games.

1975—Johnny Bucyk scores his 500th career goal.

1976—Darryl Sittler scores 10 points in 1 game.

1976—Reggie Leach scores a record-19 playoff goals.

1977—Ian Turnbull scores five goals in one game, setting a record for defensemen.

1977—Steve Shutt scores 60 goals, setting a record for left wingers.

1978—Mike Bossy becomes the first rookie to score 50 goals in 1 season.

1978—Bryan Trottier scores eight points in one game.

1979—The Montreal Canadiens win their 21st Stanley Cup.

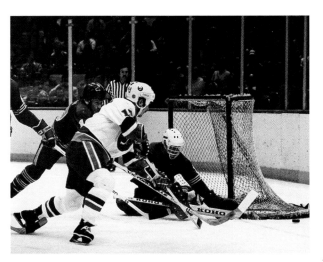

Bryan Trottier of the N.Y. Islanders.

1980—Guy Lafleur sets an NHL record with his sixth-straight 50-goal season.

1980—Garry Unger plays in his 914th consecutive game.

1981—Wayne Gretzky scores 4 goals in 1 period; also sets an NHL season record with 109 assists and 164 points.

1981—Doug Smail scores a goal five seconds into a game.

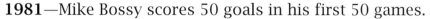

1981—Mike Bossy scores 50 goals in his first 50 games.

1983—The Edmonton Oilers score a record-424 goals in 1 season.

1983—Mark Pavelich becomes the first American-born player to score five goals in one game.

1984—Edmonton becomes the first team with three 50-goal scorers.

1984—Defenseman Paul Coffey scores 126 points in 1 season.

1984—Guy Lafleur notches his 500th career goal.

1984—Wayne Gretzky puts together an NHL-record 51-game scoring streak.

1985—Jari Kurri sets an NHL record for right wingers with 71 goals.

1985—Bobby Carpenter becomes the first American-born player to notch 50 goals in 1 season.

1986—Wayne Gretzky racks up a record 215 points and 163 assists in 1 season.

1986—Paul Coffey scores 48 goals, setting a record for defensemen.

1986—Mike Bossy scores his 500th career goal—the fastest ever.

Mike Bossy celebrates his record-making goal.

1986—Montreal wins its record-22nd Stanley Cup.

1987—Doug Jarvis plays in his 964th straight game.

1989—Mario Lemieux scores 85 goals in 1 season.

1989—Wayne Gretzky notches his 1,851st NHL point, passing Gordie Howe for the all-time record.

1989—Brian Leetch sets the mark for most goals by a rookie defenseman with 23.

1990—Bryan Trottier scores his 500th career goal.

1990—Brett Hull scores 72 goals, setting a record for right wingers.

1991—Brett Hull scores 86 goals in 1 season; also becomes the third person in NHL history to score 50 goals in less than 50 games.

1991—Rookie Ed Belfour leads the NHL in goals-against-average, save percentage, and wins.

1991—Wayne Gretzky scores his 2,000th career point and 700th career goal.

1993—Teemu Selanne scores 76 goals and 132 points in his rookie season—both NHL records.

1993—Mike Gartner records his 14th-straight 30-goal season.

Wayne Gretzky scores number 802.

1993—Montreal wins its 23rd Stanley Cup.

1993—Toronto jumps off to a 10-0-0 season start.

1994—The Florida Panthers tie an expansion team record with 33 wins in their first season.

1994—Wayne Gretzky becomes the NHL's all-time goal scorer with his 802nd career goal.

1994—Coach Scottie Bowman records his 1,000th career win.

1996—The Detroit Red Wings set a record for most wins (61) in a season.

Index